Finding Out About
VICTORIAN SCHOOLS

Amanda Clarke

Batsford Academic and Educational Ltd *London*

Contents

Typeset by Tek-Art Ltd, London SE20
and printed in Great Britain by
R.J. Acford Ltd
Chichester, Sussex
for the publishers
Batsford Academic and Educational Ltd,
an imprint of B.T. Batsford Ltd,
4 Fitzhardinge Street
London W1H 0AH

ISNB 0 7134 3667 0

ACKNOWLEDGMENTS

The Author would like to thank St Paul's Church of England Combined Schools, Leamington Spa, for use of their log books, and Hatton School, Warwick, for permission to use an Inspector's Report. Special thanks to Rosemary Booth for taking photographs of individual schools and school objects, and to Peter Clarke for his help and advice.

The Author and Publishers thank the following for their kind permission to use copyright illustrations: Rosemary Booth, page 44 (right); BBC Hulton Picture Library, pages 8, 9, 10, 12; Peter Clarke, page 44 (left); Miss P. Cole, page 41 (left); Essex Record Office, Chelmsford, page 11; The Illustrated London News Picture Library, page 7; Dr Roy A. Lowe, page 20-1 (from Seaborne and Lowe, *The English School,* Volume II, published by Routledge & Kegan Paul plc); Mansell Collection Ltd, page 31; Shakespeare Birthplace Trust Archives, page 19; Mrs S. Tuffrey, page 40; Warwickshire County Record Office, pages 18, 22, 42-3; Warwickshire Museum, frontispiece, pages 15 (Mrs F. O'Shaugnessy), 16, 17, 23, 24, 25, 26, 28 (photo by Rosemary Booth), 33, 34, 35 (photo by Rosemary Booth), 36, 37, 39.

Introduction

If you walk around any English town or village you are almost certain to come across at least one school that was built in the nineteenth century. Many of the buildings are still used as schools, some have been adapted for other uses, and some may be empty or derelict. Thousands of schools were set up during this period, but the astonishing fact is that, when Victoria came to the throne in 1837, only one third of all children went to school. At the start of her reign education was neither compulsory nor free; there was no State System and no secondary schooling for most children; and those children who actually went to school often left before reaching their teens. By 1902, however, every single child between the ages of 5 and 13 was not only entitled to a free education but was expected to attend school regularly (although it was not until 1944 that secondary schooling was made available to every child).

During the early 1800s only a small minority of the population (i.e. middle- and upper-class parents) sent their children to fee-paying schools, such as Private, Public and Grammar Schools. These children were usually from 7 to 13 years old. Although there were some schools available for poorer children, few took advantage of them, partly because the schools were few and far between, partly because parents sent their children out to work as early as possible, and partly because the general opinion was that the poorer classes did not need education.

A number of factors were responsible for the changes that slowly took place. Perhaps the most significant was the sheer number of children. In 1801 the total population of England and Wales was just under 10 million, but by 1901 it had shot up to over 32 million, with children under 14 making up between 30% and 40%. From 1851 the majority of people lived in the towns, which became grossly over-crowded, causing many families to live in appalling conditions. Vast numbers of neglected children roamed the streets, begging or thieving to keep alive. In 1847, for example, 1,272 children under the age of 12 were imprisoned for a variety of criminal offences. People became afraid of these huge numbers of children and started to think that something ought to be done about them — schooling was an answer.

Another factor responsible for change was the growing concern over child labour. Dreadful statistics and stories came to light about even tiny children having to work long hours in atrocious conditions for just a few shillings a week. Again, school seemed a better alternative.

The third factor was a general change in opinion about the education of the poor. In 1807 an MP called Davies Giddy spoke for many when he said:

> Giving education to the poor . . . would be prejudicial to their morals and happiness. It would teach them to despise their lot in life instead of making them good servants . . . in laborious employment. (The Commons Debate on Whitbreads Bill, 1807)

But the Great Reform Bill of 1832 gave many more men the vote and many thought that a proper education would give them a better understanding of politics. Charles Dickens expressed the new feeling well, in a speech to a Mechanics Institute in 1847, when he said:

> The Creator having breathed a mind into a person must have intended him to be educated.

In other words, everyone, no matter who, was entitled to an education.

Improvements were slow but steady. Various Government Acts were passed which provided grants for schools to be built in areas where they were not sufficient, and which also checked that established schools kept within a certain standard of efficiency. This system, which provided an education sponsored by and legislated for by the Government, is known as the State System. It still exists today. By the end of the nineteenth century it co-existed with the older Voluntary System of non-state schools and by 1902, between them, they provided a sound elementary education available to each child and secondary education for some.

Whilst looking at schools, we should remember the living conditions of Victorian families. It was a society of great extremes. On the one hand, there were wealthy families who lived comfortable, sheltered lives. Their children were well-fed, well-dressed and had servants to look after them. On the other hand, there were large families living in single rooms, in conditions of appalling squalor, whose children went hungry and in rags. These children were forced to work or beg merely to keep alive. For an idea of what your area might have been like in Victorian times, see if you can find any reports in newspapers of the time or from your local Board of Health (these may be in the reference section of your local library or in your County Record Office).

This book will look at the various types of schools available in Victorian times, the buildings, furniture, equipment, teachers and the children themselves. It deals mainly with Elementary Schools, which were attended by children from the ages of 5 to 13 approximately, as they were the most numerous. The book is not intended as a complete history of Victorian education, nor is it a comprehensive one. Rather, it is meant as a starting point on which to base your own research and explorations. I have extensively used my own local resources in Warwickshire, in the hope that it will encourage you to do the same in your own area and help you to become familiar with the workings of local history — in particular the history of your school.

Useful Sources

1. PLACES

a) *Schools* Many Victorian schools still exist, although not all of them are still used for the purpose for which they were built. This book will give you clues as to how to identify them (see page 44), and once you've found them, how to look at them more closely.

b) *Libraries* are a good place to start for general information. Most libraries have an education section, which includes books on the history of education. Larger libraries often have local collections which may contain information on local schools. Don't be afraid to ask the Librarian for help, and remember that, if the Library does not have the book you want, you can order it for a small fee.

c) *Museums* Some museums have objects from Victorian schooldays on display; others have actual reconstructions of schoolrooms. (See Places to Visit, page 45).

d) *Record Offices* Your teacher may be able to arrange a visit to the local Record Office, where most of the log books, accounts, building plans, reports and many more documents relating to local schools are kept. Record Offices are usually situated in the county town or in large cities. The telephone directory will tell you where your nearest one is. If you wish to visit the Record Office, you should write first of all to the County Archivist, explaining carefully what kind of material you would like to see and what subject you would like to find out about.

2. PEOPLE

a) *Head Teachers* If your school dates from the Victorian period and it is an old church school, it is just possible that the Head Teacher still has the log books. If not, he or she may still be able to give you a lot of information about the school.

b) *Elderly people* There are not many Victorians still alive, but many old people can still vividly remember their schooldays which were often very similar to Victorian times. They may be very pleased to talk to you about their childhood.

3. WRITTEN SOURCES

a) *Log books* are a fascinating and extremely informative source. In 1862 it was made compulsory for every Head Teacher of a grant-aided school to keep a weekly or daily log, in which he briefly described the activities of the school. Although teachers were specially asked not to let personal opinions enter into them, this is not usually obeyed — which is a great bonus. Log books (which are still kept today) are found in your local County Record Office or, in some cases, in the schools themselves.

b) *Directories* are useful books, which were updated annually, describing the amenities of a particular town or area. Amongst many other things, they list all the schools and often give quite detailed descriptions of them. Directories are available for most towns and counties throughout the Victorian period, and can be found in libraries and Record Offices.

c) *Books* A list of both contemporary Victorian and modern books which might be useful is given on page 46. One particularly useful book is the Victoria County History. This was a "National Historic Survey . . . designed to record the history of every county of England in detail". It was begun, but not completed, in the reign of Victoria. Your local library will house the volumes for your particular county. One volume, usually the second, will have a section of Schools. Mostly Grammar and Charity Schools, but also some Elementary Schools, are included.

d) *Old newspapers* Many libraries and Record Offices house back-copies of old-established local newspapers. Here you may find articles about the opening of a new school, or letters and articles about educational innovations.

e) *Inspectors' Reports* These are interesting and useful material and are widely available. The annual reports are written up in the log books of individual schools and often give detailed descriptions not only of the subjects taught, but also of the state of the school buildings and competence of the staff.

f) *School Board minutes and reports* Local School Boards met at least once a year, to discuss progress or otherwise in their particular area. The minutes record what was discussed at the meetings. The minutes usually come in book form and can be found at the Record Office or local library.

g) *School account books* These give a good insight into the financial side of running a school, as all expenses were recorded in them. Again, they are available either in individual schools or in Record Offices.

h) *School text books* can still be found in second-hand book shops and it's worth asking around the more elderly members of your family to see if they have kept any from their school days.

i) *Architects' plans* Each school was carefully designed by an architect and many plans still exist. They are often attractive and include both the school itself and the master's or mistress's house. Available in Record Offices.

4. VISUAL MATERIAL

a) *Old Photographs* It is surprising how many families still have photographs of relatives sitting poker-faced in some school group or austere classroom. Ask your relatives if they can help you. Museums, libraries and Record Offices also have photographic collections.

An attempt to educate children from poorer homes was made by the Sunday School Movement, which was founded in 1780 and aimed to "train the lower classes in the habits of industry and piety". Each denomination had its own schools which met once a week after church. The children were taught to read from the Bible and to behave respectfully. Children often attended Sunday Schools when they were very young — i.e. 2 or 3 years old — and might continue going until they were 12 or 13.

In 1810 further steps were taken by a Non-conformist called Joseph Lancaster, who founded the Royal Lancasterian Society which aimed to set up schools for poor children. However, his colleagues found him increasingly difficult to work with and in 1812 the society broke away from him and renamed itself the British and Foreign Schools Society. This society set up many day schools known as British Schools, which were open to all poorer children (aged about 5-13) for a small fee.

In 1811 the Church of England set up its own society called the National Society for Promoting the Education of the Poor, and this built National Schools.

Both societies depended on donations from interested people, and a small weekly fee from the children (school pence). Although the two societies were catering for the same sort of children and were using similar teaching methods, their differing religious views made them rivals throughout the century. You will often find both sorts of school in even a small town.

MONITORS

Both National and British Schools used the Monitorial System. Monitors were supposed to be the cleverest children, who were first taught by the master and were then expected to pass on the teaching to smaller groups of their own classmates. An Inspector's Report of 1845 saw drawbacks in the system:

> We cannot reflect upon the age or requirements of monitors without being struck with the absurdity of expecting good results . . . Taking the average age of monitors . . . as boys of about eleven and a half years old, reading with ease but not intelligence; writing from dictation so as to give sense of a passage but without any regard for punctuation . . . with more or less facility in working the ordinary rules of arithmetic . . . but with little or no insight into its principles. The knowledge of Geography, History and General Knowledge . . . is not called for in their employment as teachers of the lower classes.

What do you think were the advantages for the school of using monitors?

This newspaper article and picture appeared in the ▷
Illustrated London News *on 10 December 1859. The article shows with what pride a new school was received. It describes a fairly typical National School. Although there is only one building, the school is referred to as "the schools". This was because boys and girls were kept separate, both in class and in the playground, and so were regarded as being in different schools. The building is of "Gothic" or ecclesiastical style. What does this mean? Why do you think one side of the school is "rather larger than the other"?*

LEAMINGTON NATIONAL SCHOOLS.

THESE schools, which have recently been erected in the thriving town of Leamington Priors, Warwickshire, in connection with the parish church, were opened on the 3rd ult., when upwards of five hundred children partook of tea and cake. The exterior of the building has an extremely pleasing effect, being erected in a Gothic style of architecture, and presenting an elevation broken in parts, and distributed with great regard to proportion. On the roof are an ornamental bell-turret and two octagonal towers for purposes of ventilation. The whole of the building is of red brick and Bath stone, the dressed bricks being manufactured in Leamington. In the front of the building is a neat iron railing, and the open space between the railing and the schools is laid with turf and shrubs. In the interior the ornamental and the useful are blended with good taste. The length of the school-room is 77 feet by 40 feet, divided down the centre by a movable partition, so that the school-rooms are distinct on ordinary occasions, and together will accommodate 400 children, the side to the right being appropriated to the girls, and that on the left is set apart for the boys. This side of the school is rather larger than the other by about 25 feet by 17 feet, a return piece in the form of a letter L having been made use of for this additional accommodation. There are also two class-rooms, 18 feet by 15 feet, on each side of the school-rooms. A neat and convenient residence has been placed at each end for the master and mistress. Each house has a good-sized sitting-room, with bay windows; a convenient kitchen and three bed-rooms. The roof of the building is an open one, and the whole of the woodwork is stained oak colour. Gas is laid into the building, and was lighted on the occasion of the opening. The vacant land at the back of the building is divided by a wall, and forms two playgrounds, one for the boys and another for the girls; and in addition to this there is an open shed where the children may play protected from rain and other inclemencies of the weather.

7

Other Schools for Poor Children

A number of other kinds of school existed from the eighteenth century and sometimes earlier, which offered some sort of education to poor children. They varied enormously in quality and included Dame Schools, Ragged Schools, Workhouse Schools, Charity Schools and Schools of Industry. Workhouse Schools and some Industrial Schools were financed by the Poor Rate. The other kinds mentioned were set up by individuals or organizations at their own expense. They made ends meet by charging the children a few pence a week and by voluntary contributions. Charles Dickens described the sort of children these schools were trying to help:

This photograph, taken in 1857, shows the Reverend Thomas Guthrie, teaching in his Ragged School in Edinburgh. The first Ragged School was founded in 1818 and catered for children whom no other school would have — the really filthy, impoverished street urchins. The aim of these schools was to "... convert incipient criminals to Christianity". The schools were free, and they did not require their pupils to come "decently dressed". In this photograph the well-dressed girls and lady were helpers of Rev. Guthrie. By 1858 there were 192 Ragged Schools in England, teaching nearly 21,000 pauper children.

A wretched little creature who, clutching at the rags of a pair of trousers with one of its claws . . . pattered with bare feet over the muddy stones . . . . Fifty like it were about me in a moment, begging . . . clamouring, yelling, shivering in their nakedness and hunger. (*The Uncommercial Traveller*, 1861)

A WORKHOUSE SCHOOL

When families became too poor to cope and could no longer afford to rent a room or buy food, they were often sent to the workhouse. Here, husbands were often separated from wives, and children from parents. Conditions within the workhouse were bleak and comfortless, but many people were forced to spend their lives there. In 1839 there were 45,000 children living in workhouses. The 1834 Poor Law Amendment Act provided that they at least received some education:

The boys and girls who are inmates of the workhouse shall for three working hours at least each day, be instructed in Reading, Writing and Arithmetic, and in the principles of the Christian Religion; and other such instruction shall be imparted to them as may fit their service and train them to habits of usefulness, industry and virtue.

Later on, schools were actually built within workhouses.

◁ *A Dame School in about 1850, from a picture by Thomas Webster. There is a lot of activity going on, but not much learning. The Dame has her cane ready. Dame Schools were small, usually rural schools, run by elderly women. The Dame taught the children in her own home and charged a small weekly fee. Some Dames tried to teach their pupils to read and write; others merely operated a baby sitting service. Dame Schools were very common until the 1860s, when they were gradually replaced by more competent schools.*

WARWICK SCHOOL OF INDUSTRY

Children in Industrial Schools were usually taught to read and write and to do some useful trade such as sewing, carpentry, laundering or straw plaiting. The things they made were sold to the public and this contributed towards their upkeep.

White's Directory of 1850 described Warwick School of Industry:

> established about 60 years ago, by the Countess of Warwick under the patronage of whom, by the aid of subscriptions from ladies in the town and neighbourhood, is supported. Forty girls are clothed and taught reading, writing, arithmetic, sewing and knitting; the two latter are done for hire, and each girl's earnings are given to her at the end of the year. Elizabeth Cooke mistress, whose salary is £30 per annum.

How was this school financed?

A CHARITY SCHOOL IN WARWICK

Here is another extract from White's Directory of Warwickshire, 1850:

> A Charity School is held in the ancient chapel of St Peter, over the east gate of the town, in which 39 boys are taught reading, writing and arithmetic; and 36 girls reading, writing, knitting and sewing. Of these 24 boys and 24 girls are clothed in one uniform dress of blue and yellow, and are indebted to the benevolence of the late Hon Sarah Grenville for this charitable bequest; 12 girls clothed in grey, to that of Earl Brooks; 13 boys receive a coat and pair of stockings each per annum, from funds left by Mr Thomas Oken; and the expense of the other two boys by the will of the late Mr Fulk Weale. The chapel is a portion of charity left by Henry VIII, for the use of which the master pays a nominal rent of five shillings yearly. Samuel and Ann Gazey, master and mistress, whose joint salary is £70 per annum, with a house, and the privilege of taking private pupils.

Notice how this particular charity school relied on donations from several benefactors, all of whom lived at different times of history.

If you live in a town, you are almost certain to come across references to schools of these kinds. The Victoria County Histories and local directories are excellent starting points. Then perhaps you could trace the history of the school and see if the original building is still standing.

Grammar, Public and Private Schools were available throughout the Victorian period for those who could afford the fees. They were generally open for boys from middle- and upper-class backgrounds, from the age of 7 (boys were often taught at home by private tutors before this). Some Grammar Schools gave scholarships (or free places) to poor boys.

Many Grammar Schools had existed since the fifteenth century, but by the nineteenth century they were floundering, mainly because their original charters only allowed them to teach Classical subjects such as Latin and Greek Grammar. These subjects were increasingly unpopular and out-of-date in the developing industrial society of the Victorian age. The 1840 Grammar Schools Act allowed the Schools to introduce other subjects, which greatly improved their position.

The older Public Schools were introduced in the sixteenth century and were originally Grammar Schools endowed for public use. They were also meant to be controlled to some extent by a public body. However, by the nineteenth century they had become far removed from their original intentions and were generally boarding schools for upper- or middle-class boys who were trained for a life in the professions (Law, Church, Armed Forces). Discipline was lax, accommodation atrocious, teaching standards very low and the curriculum outdated. Through the work of Royal Commissions and individuals such as Dr Arnold of Rugby, vast improvements were made until, by the 1860s, Public Schools were flourishing as never before.

Private Schools abounded but varied enormously in size and quality. Some were held in private houses with only a handful of pupils and an ignorant teacher. Others were very grand, offering a wide-ranging curriculum and opulent surroundings. Local directories will give you a list of all the Private Schools in your area, while the Victoria County Histories describe any local Grammar and Public Schools there were.

This etching gives a glimpse into the schoolroom of the Lower School at Eton, perhaps our most famous Public School. The novelist William Makepeace Thackeray (1811-63) himself attended Charterhouse Public School where he was appalled at the brutality of the Public School System. In later life he wrote many articles upon the subject, and said this of life at Eton:

There are at present writing [1841] 500 boys at Eton, kicked and licked and bullied by another hundred . . . scrubbing shoes, running errands . . . and putting their posteriors on the block for Dr Hawtrey to lash at . . . . They call it the Good, Old, English System. (From The Irish Sketch Book, *1842)*

PUBLIC SCHOOLS FOUNDED IN THE VICTORIAN AGE

Here is a list of some of the Public Schools founded in the period:

Liverpool College 1840 for "the middle classes of Society".
Cheltenham College 1841 for "the sons of gentlemen".
Eltham College 1842 "for the sons of missionaries".
Marlborough 1843.
Glasgow Academy 1846.
Brighton College 1847 for "the sons of gentlemen and noblemen".
Radley College, Oxon 1847.
Hurstpierpoint 1850.
Clifton College, Bristol 1861.
Haileybury, Herts 1862.
Framlingham College, Suffolk 1864.
Kelly College, Tavistock 1867.
The Leys, Cambridge 1871.
Wrekin College, Salop 1884.
Abbotsholme, Derby 1889.

Where were the majority of them situated?

Private Schools

This photograph taken at the end of the nineteenth century ▷ shows how one Grammar School, King Edward VI Grammar School in Chelmsford, Essex, had fully incorporated Science into its curriculum. A new science school was added to the original buildings in 1899, at a cost of £800. It included a lecture theatre (illustrated), a physics laboratory, an optical room and balance room. Adult evening classes were also held there.

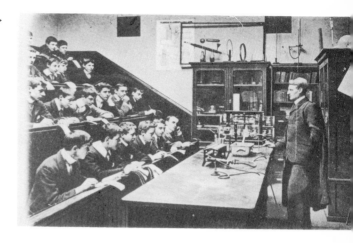

BIRMINGHAM GRAMMAR SCHOOL

Free Grammar, or King Edward's School, New Street was founded by King Edward the VI, in the fifth year, (1552), of his reign, and endowed with the revenue of the Guild of the Cross, which prior to the Dissolution, occupied the site of the present building .... The management is vested in a bailiff and 18 governors, who appoint a head master, second master, and usher, with a writing master and a drawing master .... The governors have recently obtained an act to enable them to appoint masters to teach mathematics, modern languages, and arts and sciences in the grammar school .... An annual visitation of the school is held, at which three resident members of the universities attend and examine the boys, and report upon the state of the school to the governors. There are 10 exhibitions of £50 a year each, for 4 years attached to this school; they are open to any college, and are given by the governors to the boys who are declared by the examiners to be highest in classical attainment. (White's Directory of Warwickshire, 1850)

What sort of institution do you think the Guild of the Cross was? Which act allowed Grammar Schools to widen their curriculum?

LEAMINGTON COLLEGE

Leamington College was a Private School in Leamington Spa, Warwickshire:

This establishment was founded in 1841, with the view of providing the sons of the Nobility, Gentry and Clergy with a sound, classical and mathematical education, in accordance with the Christian principles of the Established Church. The course of instruction included the Hebrew, Greek, Latin, English and German tongues, Mathematics, Civil engineering and fortification .... It is constructed on the most approved plans and heated throughout with hot water. There is a bathroom .... Each boy has a separate sleeping apartment on the cubic principle, and the older boys private studies. (White's Directory, 1872).

For a description of a really different Private School, read *Nicholas Nickleby* by Charles Dickens, where one of the attractions of the grim Dotheboys Hall was that it allowed no holidays.

Education for Girls

At the beginning of Victoria's reign most people agreed with the saying that "A woman's place is in the home", and girls from all classes were taught to believe in and prepare themselves for such an existence. It was thought that the only accomplishments a girl needed were ones that would get her a good husband, and enable her to run a home.

While their brothers were away at Private or Public School, girls from the upper and middle classes were often taught at home by governesses; or they were sent to Private Schools for "young ladies". They learnt such things as drawing, needlework, painting, household management and a spattering of cultural subjects such as French and Literature.

Girls from working-class families were taught by their mothers and had a less refined "curriculum" based on laundrywork, baby-minding and cooking. Or they went to the same elementary schools as their brothers and shared the same timetable, but often with greater emphasis being placed on needlework than on mathematics.

Not only was too much learning considered unladylike, but girls were also thought to be less intelligent than boys. However, attitudes slowly changed, partly thanks to the work of two women, Dorothea Beale and Frances Buss, who opened their own secondary schools for girls, run on similar lines to the schools for boys.

The Royal Commission of 1895, known as the Bryce Report, enquired into the state of secondary education, but it paid special attention to the situation of girls. Women Commissioners were especially appointed.

The table below comes from the Bryce Report. It compares the curriculum of four girls' schools in the West Riding of Yorkshire.

Bradford Class II	Keighley Class V	Leeds Class II	Sheffield Class V
Hrs per week Scripture ½ History 2 Geog. 2 English 6¾ French 2¼ Needlework 2 PE 1 Singing 1 Drawing 1	Scripture 1 History 1 Geog. 1½ English 7¼ French 1 Needlework 1½ PE 1¼ Physical Science 1 Singing 1 Drawing 1	Scripture 1 History 1¼ Geog. ¾ Reading 1½ Dictation 1 French 1¾ Latin 1¼ Drawing 1 Geometrical Drawing ½ Gymnastics 2 Natural Science 1 Singing 2	Scripture 1½ History 2 Geog. 1½ English 2¾ French 2 Needlework ¾ PE 1 Object Lesson ¾ Singing ¾ Drawing 1½

Although the Commission found that every girl should be encouraged to prepare herself for some definite career, the old attitudes still remained, for the same lady Commissioner also recommended:

It must be borne in mind the best curriculum suited for them [girls] is not quite the same as for boys .... Girls, no matter what may be their social status, have always to prepare themselves to some extent for home life ....

A girls' private school out for a walk, early 1900s.

She suggested that girls should be taught the following:

... cookery, laundrywork, and domestic management based on a scientific knowledge of Chemistry and the Laws of Health ... needlework in conjunction with drawing, designing, colouring and artistic training generally. Arithmetic should be retained but taught in a commercial aspect with its bearing upon account keeping and book keeping.

Do we still agree with this today? How and why do you think attitudes have changed?

Grants and the Revised Code

The Newcastle Commission was set up in 1858 to

> inquire into the present state of popular education in England and to consider and report what measures if any are required for the extension of a sound and cheap elementary instruction to all classes of people.

It concluded:

> There is only one way of securing this result which is to institute a searching examination by competent authority of every child in every school in which grants are to be paid . . . and to make the position of the teacher depend to a considerable extent on the results of this examination.

The Commission proposed that Government grants should be based on regular attendance, good exam results and a report by an Inspector.

Many of the Newcastle Commission's recommendations were carried out in the Revised Code of 1862. This provided for "Payment by Results". Basically, the Government paid every grant-aided school a maximum grant of 12 shillings for each child — 4 shillings for regular attendance and 8 shillings for passes in exams in the "Three Rs" (i.e. 2/8 for each subject passed). Only a pass in a subject got a grant.

At first, grants were only available for the "Three Rs", but in 1867 "specific subjects" became grantable. These included Geography, History and English. In 1875 "class" subjects such as needlework were also included. In 1890 one basic grant was awarded for Elementary Schools, and in 1897 exams were abolished, but HMIs still made surprise visits. The whole system was ended in 1901.

What do you think the advantages and disadvantages of such a system were? How do you think the teachers felt about it?

The traditional view of the Government regarding education was one of "laissez-faire"; the idea was that people were responsible for their own lives and so, if they wanted their children educated, they should be left to provide the means. The Government would not interfere. Similarly, the schools were expected to find their own funds. However, by the 1830s it was obvious that few schools could exist on voluntary contributions alone. In 1833 the first Government grant to the voluntary societies was awarded, for the "Erection of School Houses for the Education of the Children of the Poorer Classes in Great Britain". Gradually, the Government became more and more involved. Grants were awarded annually and Inspectors were appointed to make sure that they were spent correctly. In 1839 the Committee of Council for Education was founded, which later became the Department of Education. A Royal Commission was set up in the 1850s to see how well children were being taught and whether money could be saved, and this eventually resulted in the Revised Code of 1862, which was to have a profound effect on education.

The Bryce Report of 1895 included this table showing the ages of boys in the different standards of Leeds Higher Grade School, October 1894. By this time a Standard VII had been added (see page 20). Earlier on in the century, very few children would have stayed on at school after the age of 13. Many left much younger.

How do you think the 13-year-old felt, being in the same class as some of the children under 8? Do you think this system, based on ability, was a fair one?

EXTRACT FROM THE REVISED CODE

Every scholar for whom grants are claimed must be examined according to one of the following standards:

	STANDARD I	STANDARD II	STANDARD III
Reading	Narrative in mono-syllables	One of the Narratives next in order after monosyllables in an elementary reading book used in the school.	A short paragraph from an elementary reading book used in the school.
Writing	Form on blackboard or slate, from dictation, letters, capital and small manuscript.	Copy in manuscript character a line of print.	A sentence from the same paragraph, slowly read once, and then dictated in single words.
Arithmetic	Form on black-board or slate, from dictation, figures up to 20; name at sight figures up to 20; add and subtract figures up to 10, orally, from ex-amples on black-board	A sum in simple addition or subtrac-tion, and the multi-plication table.	A sum in any simple rule as far as short division (inclusive).

	STANDARD IV	STANDARD V	STANDARD VI
Reading	A short paragraph from a more ad-vanced reading book used in the school.	A few lines of poetry from a reading book used in the first class of the school.	A short ordinary para-graph in a news-paper, or other modern narrative.
Writing	A sentence slowly dictated once by a few words at a time, from the same book, but not from the paragraph read.	A sentence slowly dictated once, by a few words at a time, from a reading book used in the first class of the school.	Another short ordi-nary paragraph in a newspaper, or other modern narrative, slowly dictated once by a few words at a time.
Arithmetic	A sum in compound rules (money).	A sum in compound rules (common weights and measures).	A sum in practice or bills of parcels.

This extract from the Revised Code gives a good idea of how thorough the examinations were. For the purposes of the examination, children were divided into Standards or classes, of which there were six. Although these were based on age, children could only go up a standard if they passed the annual exam. If they failed, they stayed where they were. This meant that there were often children of mixed ages in one class.

				Standard			
	I	II	III	IV	V	VI	VII
8	7	5					
	5	16	8				
	—	15	24	21			
	—	8	21	40	21	5	
	—	1	9	31	48	34	4
	—	1	1	19	41	97	80
	—	—	—	2	6	17	38
	—	—	—	—	7	12	

Under 12   322
Over 12   532

GRANT FOR ST PAUL'S SCHOOL LEAMINGTON SPA, 1868

This extract from the 1867 log book of St Paul's Church of England Combined Schools shows how the grants were worked out:

99 boys present
53 boys presented for examination

6 Classes

6th	17
5th	15
4th	6
3rd	9
2nd	3
1st	3
Infant	1

41 passed all 3Rs	
11 passed 2 subjects	
1 passed 1 subject	
Passes in Standards 1-3	38
Passes in Standards 4-6	108
Total:	146
Number for payment at 2/8d	146
Number for payment at 6/6	1

Average attendance	
Under 6 years of age	2
Over 6 years of age	64
Total	66

Grants Claimable for 1868	£	s	d
On average attendance (66 @ 4/-)	13	4	0
On examination (146 @ 2/8)	19	9	4
On infants present (1)		6	6
Gross total of claim	32	19	10

Infants present on the day of examination were automatically granted 6/6d. Notice that not all child-ren were put in for examination.

15

Inspectors and Examinations

The first of Her Majesty's Inspectors (HMIs) of schools were appointed in 1840 to make sure that the Government grants were being spent correctly. After the Revised Code of 1862, HMIs also visited every grant-aided school to take the annual examination. Each child was tested in the 3Rs, the attendance record was checked, the buildings looked over and the teacher's log book read. Examination-day was one of foreboding because the teachers' salaries depended on how many children they got through the exam. Sick children were brought in for the day and classes were drilled parrot-fashion with possible questions and answers. Cheating was not unknown!

Inspectors' Reports were written into the school log book. Here is the Report on Hatton Junior School, Warwick, 1871.

AN INSTRUCTION TO INSPECTORS, 1840

At first, before the Revised Code, Inspectors were supposed to be helpful to the schools, not just critical. The minutes of the Committee of Council for Education in August 1840 pointed out that:

> . . . The Inspector is not intended as a means of exercising control but of affording assistance . . . . An important part of [his] duties will consist in visiting from time to time, schools aided by grants of public money . . . in order to ascertain that the grant in each case has been duly applied . . . . [They should also check] . . . as to manners and behaviour, whether orderly and decorous, as to obedience whether prompt and cheerful . . . and as to rewards and punishments on what principles administered and with what results.

Hatton School (Warwick)

Boys." The general efficiency of this school is pretty fair - The supply of books, is hardly sufficient - a second Reading book is much wanted

Girls. This school has been managed by a mother & daughter: the daughter is now recognized as the responsible mistress. The buildings are very good. The desks are fair - insufficient for the number of girls - Reading, writing dictation & needlework fair - Arithmetic moderate —

Flora Thompson was born in 1876 in Juniper Hill, on the borders of Oxfordshire and Northamptonshire. Her autobiography, *Lark Rise to Candleford* describes life in her village in about 1887. She uses the pseudonym Fordlow National School for the school she attended. Here,

Compare Flora's description with the words of a school song from an Elementary School in Wiltshire in the 1880s:

Would you like to know the reason
Why we all look so bright and gay
As we hasten to our places?
This is our Inspection Day!
You know we've done our duty,
Duly striving with all might,
Teacher says we need not worry
Though our sums will not come right.
So we are glad and gay
Though 'tis Inspection Day.

Her Majesty's Inspector of Schools came once a year on a date of which previous notice had been given. There was no singing or quarrelling on the way to school that morning. The children in clean pinafores and well blacked boots, walked deep in thought or with open spelling or table book in hand, tried to make up for in an hour all their wasted yesterdays.

When a child passed a certain standard, he or she was presented with a very smart certificate. Can you find which standard this child has passed?

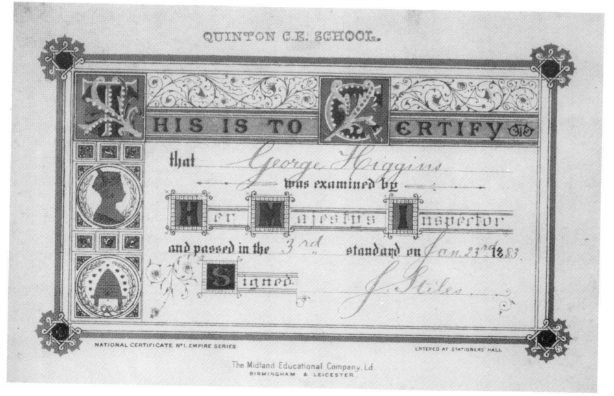

QUINTON C.E. SCHOOL.

THIS IS TO CERTIFY that *George Higgins* was examined by Her Majesty's Inspector and passed in the 3rd standard on Jan 23rd 1883. Signed. *J. Stiles.*

NATIONAL CERTIFICATE Nº1. EMPIRE SERIES   ENTERED AT STATIONERS' HALL

The Midland Educational Company, Ld
BIRMINGHAM & LEICESTER.

The 1870 Education Act

By the 1860s the general opinion was that education was a right, not a privilege. However, there were still large numbers of children who did not go to school. The 1870 Education Act aimed to remedy this. The whole country was divided up into areas, and each area was examined to see how many children there were and how many school places were available. Those areas that had too few places were expected to appoint School Boards, and these Boards were then to be responsible for building new schools where there were none and for restoring the standards of existing schools, which were invited to join the Board. The schools which belonged to the Board were called Board Schools.

The School Boards could levy rates to pay for the schools, and decided whether education was to be compulsory in their area. Board Schools were only allowed to provide general Christian teaching — not to give religious instruction according to the ideas of the Church of England or any other group. All parents could then send their children to Board Schools and any who were not Christian could ask to have their children taken out of Prayers and R.I. lessons.

National and British Schools were given six months to either improve their own schools or come in with the new Boards. Many National Schools refused to join because of the religious clause — they thought that only Anglican-based religion should be taught — and this led to what was known as the Dual System. On the one hand, there were the Board Schools supported by the State, receiving grants, rates and school pence; while, on the other hand, there were the Church Schools which still existed on endowments and grants from any exams they took.

As a result of the 1870 Act, even the remotest areas came to have their own schools and education did at least become available to all. Schooling was eventually made compulsory up to the age of 10 by the Acts of 1876 and 1880, and an Act of 1891 made it free.

The Leamington School Board was set up in March 1881. Until then, the town must have managed to continue to provide education through voluntary contributions. The new School Board sent a letter like this to all the schools in its area. Spencer Street was a Congregational school for boys founded in 1840. It became Spencer Street Board School.

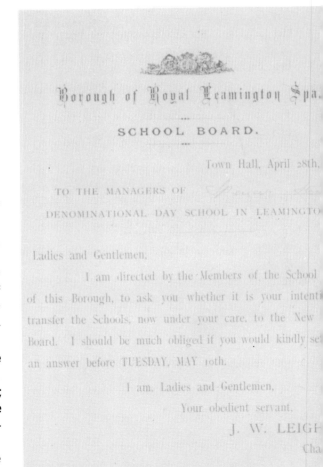

This poster was issued by the Stratford on Avon burgesses, who supported the National Schools and were therefore unwilling for them to join the new Board. Their argument is founded on expenses — pointing out that National Schools are far more economical to run. ▷

LEAMINGTON'S BOARD SCHOOLS

The Leamington School Board's Triennial Report for 1884-87 said:

> The education given in Board schools is of a strictly elementary nature in character and in accord with the requirements of the Government Code, with the exception of drawing in the Boys' Schools where required, and Domestic Cookery in the Girls' School .... The fullest Religious Instruction allowed by the Act is given. The Scriptures are read daily, school is opened and closed with a prayer and specially selected hymns are sung by the children. The policy of the School Board has been to impart a thorough knowledge to the children and to discountenance a high class education for the benefit of a few at the cost of the ratepayers.

What does the Report seem to think is important in education?

THE SCHOOL BOARD MEETING
TO-NIGHT.

FELLOW BURGESSES,

The School Board was originated last March by the Education Department to see that our Children received proper education, but the individual members of it were elected by us Burgesses to see that such education was given at the least possible expense.

At present school room is not provided for the number of children the Department have fixed, and the School Board will have to provide for the deficiency at our expense unless the offers which have been made to the Board to find it, free of charge to the ratepayers, are accepted.

It is estimated that Schools built by School Boards cost about £10 for every child, while we know that the Managers of the National Schools have built for 175 children at less than £4 10 per child, or less than half the money which the Ratepayers must have paid if the Managers had not built.

The School Board has told us that there are 1265 children educated at the various Schools, of which 791 go to the National Schools and 192 to the Board School.

The Reports of the National Schools show that to educate their 791 children the Managers have to collect about £160.

For the School Board a Rate of 3½d in the £, which brings in more than £350, has just been collected.

A comparison of these figures shows that every child educated in the National Schools costs the subscribers 4s., while in the Board School each child costs the Ratepayers £1 16s. 6d.

If the Board had to educate all the 1,265 children it would cost us annually over £2,300, or a 2s. rate, in addition to a very heavy rate for building Schools.

21st November, 1881.

A BURGESS.

PUPILS AT A LONDON BOARD SCHOOL

James Runciman (1852-91) was a Pupil Teacher at North Shields Ragged School. He later qualified and taught at several schools in the London Board area. In his book, *Schools and Scholars* (1887) he described some of his London pupils:

> They were a wild lot gathered in the Willow Alley Shed .... Most of the little fellows had been used to blows .... Some were cowed and shy but vicious and some were dulled into semi-imbecility by hunger, disease and ill-usage .... The teacher found it impossible to interest them in any subject for more than five minutes.

19

Secondary Education

For most of the nineteenth century the majority of children left school before they reached their teens, the exceptions being those who were educated privately or at Grammar Schools. By the 1890s there was growing support for the idea of secondary education, that is, something more than elementary instruction, being available to more children. One way of achieving this was by adding a seventh standard to the Elementary Schools (i.e. the Church and Board Schools). Another way was by introducing special Higher Grade Schools, which catered for older children. A third way was to provide more scholarships for clever children to attend Grammar and Public Schools.

The Taunton Commission of 1864-68 had investigated, amongst other things, the state of secondary education and found it very lacking, but it was the report of the Bryce Commission of 1895 which led to the main changes. The Bryce Commission looked specifically at secondary education and its recommendations were finally carried out in the 1902 Education Act.

The 1902 Act introduced Local Education Authorities (LEAs), which replaced the old School Boards. The LEAs were responsible for building new Secondary Schools and Teacher Training Colleges. (Clever children now sat a scholarship examination and those who did well enough went on to a Secondary School.) The LEAs were also responsible for Elementary Schools and were allowed to give grants to Church Schools where required. They introduced a wider curriculum into their schools, which included Mathematics, Science, Geography and History.

The LEAs remain the basis of our education system today.

This photograph shows Varna Street Board Schools, Gorton, Manchester, which had a "Higher" section. Compare it with some of the other schools in the book and you will get a good idea of the variety in design and size that Victorian schools achieved.

SECONDARY EDUCATION AT THE HALIFAX HIGHER BOARD SCHOOL

The Bryce Report included these extracts from the curriculum of the Halifax Higher Board School:

First Year [i.e. about 13 years old]
English: A period of English history and literature; and the study of an English Classic.
Latin: Latin grammar and elementary composition; easy translation.
Mathematics: Arithmetic; algebra; Euclid.

Science: Inorganic chemistry (theoretical and practical); sound, light and heat.
French: Thorough revision of grammar; easy translation.
Drawing: Practical plane and solid geometry; freehand.
Commercial: Shorthand; geography (British Islands, Australia and British North America), book keeping.
Manual instructions in the workshop.
Gymnastics.

Fourth Year [i.e. about 17 years old]
English: History of the English language; modern literature and history.
Latin: Caesar; De Bello Gallico, Book VII; Roman history and geography.
Mathematics: Algebra; Euclid; trigonometry; solid geometry and conic sections.
French: Grammar; Racine, Athalie; Sardou, La Perle Noire.
German: Grammar; conversation; Lange's German Reader.
Science: Theoretical mechanics (advanced); inorganic chemistry (hons.); physiography (advanced); botany; machine construction.
Art: mechanical drawing; shading from objects and casts; painting in water colours and oils.
Manual instruction in the workshop.
Gymnastics.

The school was for boys only.

Make a list of all the subjects you learn at school, and then see how it compares. Some of the subjects might be the same but have different names. See if you can find a sixth former's timetable and see how that compares with the higher standard.

School Buildings

An enormous number of schools were built during the Victorian period and many of them are still in use today. To begin with, they usually consisted of a single schoolroom where all the children were taught together. Sometimes the schoolroom was partitioned by curtains or screens to make smaller rooms, so that the different standards could be taught separately. Later, schools were built with a schoolroom and several smaller classrooms, as well as houses for the master or mistress. Playgrounds were a later luxury. Boys and girls were normally separated, both in and out of school, and had their own entrances. Inside the school, facilities were very basic. The schoolroom was tall and draughty and the windows were purposely high to that the children could not look out. Heating was by open fires or smelly stoves, and ventilation was a constant problem. Lighting was by gas lights or oil lamps.

ST MARY'S PAROCHIAL SCHOOLS, LEAMINGTON

Becks Leamington Guide of 1845 describes the interior of this school which was built in 1842:

> The schoolrooms are of recent construction and together with the Mistress' house cost at least £1200. The interior is spacious and well adapted for the purpose it is designed, being capable of containing 500 persons. Its dimensions are at least 68ft in length, by 23ft wide, and from the ceiling are suspended two chandeliers, each bearing 3 gas burners elegantly fitted up . . . . The building is divided into two equal parts by an oak partition, over which a drapery of crimson moreen descends from the roof . . . one partition being appropriated to the boys and the other to the girls.

How light do you think it would have been in this school?

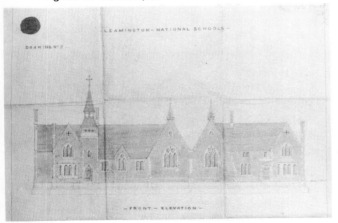

◁ This is an architect's plan of a National School, which was eventually opened in 1859. (The finished school is described on page 7.) The design is typically "churchy". Plans like these are usually found in County Record Offices.

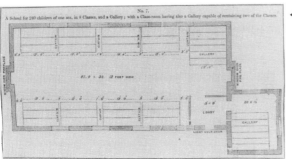

◁ This plan for a school is taken from a book by E.R. Robson on School Architecture (1880s) and shows a very common design. Notice that the schoolroom is partitioned only by curtains. There are two galleries — small lecture theatres which were good for teaching large numbers of children at once, for everybody, no matter where they sat, could see what was going on. You can see a gallery in the picture on page 11.

Many open fires and stoves were far from perfect, but the manufacturers of the Boyd School Grate (pictured in Robson's book) thought that this was the ideal sort of heating for a school.

This design (again pictured in Robson's book) is for a rather superior cloakroom with washbasins. Few schools would have had this.

NEW VENTILATION SYSTEM AT CHILVERS COTON SCHOOL WARWICKSHIRE

The log book of Chilvers Coton School for 1891 recorded:

March 12 During this week the ventilation of the school has been attended. Five new inlets (Tobin's Tubes) have been put in. Three large outlets have been provided which are guaranteed to prevent all draught.

May 15 The ventilation arrangements answer admirably. As this week has been very warm the improvements have been noticeable. Formerly owing to the oppressive unhealthy atmosphere, afternoon school used to be very difficult as the air rendered the boys dull, lazy and listless. Now they work with much more vigour and good order is more easily obtained.

FLORA THOMPSON'S SCHOOL, OXFORDSHIRE

Flora Thompson described the building of Fordlow National School in *Lark Rise to Candleford*:

Fordlow National School was a small, one storey building, standing at the crossroads to the entrance to the village. The one large classroom which served all purposes, was well lit with several windows including the large one which filled the end of the building which faced the road. Besides and joined to the school was a tiny two roomed cottage for the School Mistress, and beyond that a playground with birch trees . . . the whole being enclosed within pointed, white pailings.

What aspects of modern school-buildings do you think would most surprise a Victorian child today?

Furniture and Equipment

Compared with our well-equipped modern schools, Victorian classrooms would strike us as very bleak and sparsely furnished. The floors and walls were often bare, the wooden seats hard, uncomfortable and cramped, and the atmosphere stuffy and probably rather smelly. The teacher usually had a large, formidable desk at the front of the class, while the rest of the furniture consisted of a cupboard, blackboard and easel. Equipment depended on how wealthy the school was. Most had a supply of slates and pencils, limited text books and paper. Others had globes, abacus, charts and object lesson boxes.

A REQUEST FOR MORE MATERIALS

On 31 October 1882 C.E. Stuart, a teacher at Nethersole's Foundation School, Polesworth, Tamworth, wrote to the Rev. H. Hammer, asking for more material:

At present I am quite out of pens, pen and pencil holders, slates, copybooks, exercise books and double small foolscap. I am aware that the list is a long one . . . but I shall be very careful with the books . . . so that they will last for three or four years at least . . . . The maps are necessary for teaching class subjects and would be in use for at least one hour ten minutes per week . . . . I have only one easel in the school. . . two easels are requisite but having a double faced one will answer for all the schools requirements . . . . I most earnestly pray you will allow me to have them otherwise I cannot do duty to you and the school or justice to myself.

Rev. Hammer was probably a Manager of the school. In his place, would you have answered C.E. Stuart's request?

This very bleak schoolroom pictured in E.R. Robson's book, School Architecture *(1880s) has been partitioned down the middle. There is nothing on the walls and the only equipment the teachers seem to have are two desks and a blackboard. What sort of lighting does the room have? Compare this picture with other pictures of classrooms in this book and see if they were always this bleak.*

Robson's School Architecture *showed this double- ▷ sided blackboard. It is also on wheels so that it could be easily moved. Why would it have needed to be moved?*

MATERIALS RECEIVED

The log book for 1902 of Chilvers Coton School for Boys, Warwickshire, recorded:

> October 24: Received one gross lead pencils, 3lbs India Rubber, 1 gross drawing pins, 3000 sheets of squared drawing paper and a set of chemical apparatus and some chemicals.

How can you tell that this isn't likely to be an extract from early in the nineteenth century?

A "VERY SATISFACTORY SCHOOL"

The HMI's report for 1853-54 was praising of St Peter's Roman Catholic School for Boys, Leamington Spa:

> Boys' classroom excellent, Offices good — four in parallel rows against the wall. Furniture — two cupboards, two grates, desk, table. Books in sufficient supply. . . . Apparatus good . . . . Discipline good . . . well organised. Three classes for three subjects in semi circles with collective groups for geography. Under Master and one apprentice . . . . A very satisfactory school of its class, taught with assiduity and intelligence.

THE ARRANGEMENT OF CLASSES

A booklet published by the Committee of Council for Education in 1885 gave advice on the arrangement of classes. For example:

> No group [of desks] should contain more than three rows of benches and desks. Each group of desks must be separated . . . by an alley for the passage of the children . . . . Alleys should be 18ins wide. An allowance of 18ins on each desk and bench will suffice for the junior classes, but not less than 22ins may be allowed for the senior classes.
> An easel and blackboard should be provided for each class, and a larger black-board for the gallery.
> No Infant gallery should hold more than 80 or 90 infants.
> The time table of the school should be arranged as the classes engaged in comparatively silent occupations (such as writing, slate arithmetic, drawing, committing to memory and the like) may always be interspersed between classes that are reading or receiving instruction.

Does the double classroom pictured here seem to have followed these rules?

Teachers and Their Helpers

During the first half of the nineteenth century literally anyone could open a school or offer their services as a school teacher. As there was no training scheme, teachers were at best satisfactory, or at worst grossly incompetent — there were, of course, a few notable exceptions. There was often only one teacher to a school, and so he or she found himself or herself confronting over a hundred children. Discipline must have been very difficult, and the sheer size of the classes made rote learning the only possible method of teaching. Monitors (page 6) provided a little help, as the teacher could divide the class into more manageable groups.

In 1846 the Pupil Teacher System was introduced by Sir James Kay-Shuttleworth, Secretary of the Committee of Council for Education, in order

> to raise the character and position of the Schoolmaster . . . to render the school popular among the Poor, as a means of introducing their children to more profitable and honourable employment . . . to create in the minds of the Working Class a juster estimate of the value of education for their children.

At the age of 13, Pupil Teachers began a five-year apprenticeship. If they completed that successfully, they could then go on to Teacher Training College, where, providing they passed the course, they then became "certificated" teachers. If they only did moderately well as apprentices, they were often kept on at the school and known as "Assistants".

An Infant School with their teacher and Pupil Teacher, at the beginning of the twentieth century. The children are sitting in a gallery. What do you notice about the styles of their clothes?

PROBLEMS WITH PUPIL TEACHERS

The log books of St Paul's Church of England Combined Schools, Leamington Spa, record some problems:

March 8 1869 The Pupil Teacher complains that teaching makes his head ache.

May 12 1876 John P, Pupil Teacher, was absent on Thursday . . . and Friday owing to a severe bilious attack.

1877, Committee Minutes Mr W opened the meeting by stating that grave insubordination had taken place among the Pupil Teachers . . . the girls denied everything but the boys confessed to having romped with them and kissed the girl teachers.

Salaries were very variable, depending on age, sex and, after the Revised Code, results of the annual examination. Generally speaking, teachers were poorly paid, though they often got a free school house to live in. Here are some examples of salaries from Elementary Schools:

1850

Master, certificated	£88	5s 2d
Master, uncertificated	£57	11s 3d

1881

Headmaster	£100	0s 0d
Pupil Teacher	£17	0s 0d
Pupil Teacher	£15	0s 0d

1881

Headmistress	£50	0s 0d
Assistant	£48	0s 0d
Pupil Teacher	£16	0s 0d
Pupil Teacher	£14	0s 0d
Monitor	£7	16s 0d

What do you notice about the women's salaries? Would it be allowed today?

SCHOOL MISTRESS WANTED

This advertisement for a School Mistress appeared in a Warwickshire paper in 1865:

> Wanted for an endowed Girls School, not under Government, a Mistress of sound church principles (certificate not absolutely necessary) unmarried, a good knowledge of cutting out and needlework desirable, will be required to teach in Sunday School; and a knowledge of music will be a recommendation. Must be healthy and energetic. Remuneration £40pa payable quarterly by the Trustees. A very good house free from payment ... £5pa is allowed for school coal. None but thoroughly well qualified persons need apply and a personal interview will be required.

What does "not under Government" mean? How was this school heated?

Many girls became teachers, as it was one of the few professions regarded as "respectable", although they were often regarded as "blue-stockings".

Children in School

Victorian children lived in a society of extremes. The developing educational system had to cater for everyone, which meant that some children went to school well-dressed and well-fed, whilst others arrived dirty and hungry. However, once in school, the routine was much the same.

Many children started school when they were only three and they joined an Infant School. They went on to Elementary School at the age of six or seven, and after the 1880s, it was possible for a few lucky children to go on to a Technical or Secondary School at the age of eleven, twelve or thirteen.

Elementary School would begin at nine o'clock, there was a two-hour break from twelve noon until two, and school continued until four or five in the afternoon. Few schools provided meals, so children brought a snack with them or went home to lunch. Most children also attended Sunday School.

Children were expected to behave well at all times, both at home and at school. They were expected to be polite, speak only when spoken to and show respect to their "elders and betters", who included their school teachers. Any misdemeanours — and, judging by the log books, Victorian children were just as mischievous as today's — were swiftly dealt with, either by a severe reprimand or by a caning. "Spare the rod and spoil the child" was a well-known and much-believed Victorian saying. On the other hand, children who were well-behaved were rewarded with medals, pictures or carefully selected books.

A back straightener was designed to make "lazy" children sit upright. It was worn when a child was sitting down and working. It must have been very uncomfortable, but Victorians thought good "deportment" very important.

CLOTHING

Flora Thompson also described the children's clothes,

. . . the girls in their ankle length frocks and long, straight pinafores with their hair strained back from their brows and secured on their crowns by a ribbon or black tape or a bootlace. The bigger boys in corduroys and hob-nailed boots, and the smaller ones in home made sailor suits or until they were six or seven in petti-coats.

Compare this description with the picture on page 26-27.

WALKING TO SCHOOL

Children from rural areas often had to walk to school. In *Lark Rise to Candleford* Flora Thompson remembers that if it was cold,

some of them carried two hot potatoes, which had been in the oven, or in the ashes all night, to warm their hands on the way, and to serve as a light lunch on arrival.

(Lunch was a mid-morning snack; dinner was eaten at mid-day.)

PRANKS AND PUNISHMENTS

The log books of St Paul's Church of England Combined Schools, Leamington Spa, record:

June 8 1863 George L, a scholar, by means of a key opened the master's desk during dinner time . . . and abstracted three shillings and one half penny. Several children saw him do this, and the case being so clearly proved he was dismissed from the school as punishment to himself and an example to the other scholars.

July 24 1863 Spoke to several boys on the subject of coming to school with clean hands and faces, and of combing and cleaning the head, a necessity fast becoming a rarity.

November 5 1863 One of the boys formerly of this school met with a severe accident — an explosion of gunpowder.

April 13 1864 One of the Infant Class pushed a pea into his ear, excitement of the whole class — after some time it was extricated.

October 3 1865 C, a little boy from the First Standard put in prison for a night for stealing from gardens. Appears thoroughly frightened.

August 6 1867 Obscene language discovered in the closet. Cautioned the whole school.

February 24 1868 A dog ran into the school hiding under some benches behind the little ones, caused great confusion.

August 20 1868 A lady complained of A . . . being allowed to run about barefoot, begging.

August 21 1868 Found two boys in the Second Standard eating pigs hoofs — a detestable habit.

October 20 1870 Mrs D (an Irishwoman) brought her two sons to be flogged — prescribing as an effectual remedy for truant playing, reading verses of the Scriptures, with a stripe at the conclusion of each, on the back with a stout cane.

March 13 1876 Punished the Sixth Standard for irreverence during singing.

Other causes to punish children included sending Valentines, throwing snowballs, breaking glass in a greenhouse, making April Fools and chasing an "unruly beast" down the street!
     Which of the misdeeds in the extracts do you think deserved the greatest punishment?

REWARD FOR GOOD BEHAVIOUR

In most schools good behaviour was also made an example:

April 20 1863 Rev JB called and in the presence of the whole school presented William B with a certificate card of good conduct and half a crown in money. The said William B's conduct in school good and industrious. (St Paul's Church of England Combined Schools, log book)

In 1870 School Boards could make attendance at school compulsory if they wanted to, until an Act of 1876 finally made elementary education compulsory for each child up to the age of ten. By 1902 the minimum school-leaving age was thirteen. Generally speaking, this meant that from 1870 onwards most children were at school for somewhere between five and ten years. However, getting children to come to school and stay there was a constant problem. Many School Boards appointed Attendance Officers whose job was to find out the children who weren't coming to school and make sure that they did in the future. For persistent non-attendance, children could ultimately be brought before the courts and their parents fined.

REASONS FOR ABSENCE

Children could be absent from school for many reasons. We can divide them up into categories. These examples all come from the log books of St Paul's Church of England Combined Schools, Leamington Spa, Warwickshire.

Illness

October 23 1863 Several children ill through eating noxious compounds of sweets sold at small shops.

February 26 1865 Whooping cough prevalent among the smaller children.

May 6 1865 Several children ill through drinking bad water.

October 3 1896 School closed on account of measles (the closure lasted for six weeks).

Epidemics such as measles, chicken pox, scarlet fever, diphtheria and whooping cough swept through schools annually, causing many children to be absent. Some even died. Why are conditions so much better today?

Work

September 12 1864 Attendance gradually decreasing. Boys getting in acorns for the pigs. Others as errand boys.

March 25 1865 Several boys sent messages saying they were unable to come [to school] . . . working in the brickyards.

At harvest time children were often kept away to help their parents, for there were many jobs that even quite small children could do.

Distractions

August 7 1863 Cautioned boys against attending the races held at Warwick.

September 14 1864 A Statute Fair [Mop] at Kenilworth causing a thin attendance.

May 29 1865 Militia in the cricket field. Thin attendance.

Bad weather also caused fluctuations in attendance, as sometimes it was too snowy for the children to get to school, or occasionally the children were actually sent home as it was too cold to work in the class-rooms.

FINES FOR NON-ATTENDANCE

The Triennial Report of the Leamington School Board reported:

> During 1881, 86 summonses were taken out against parents for not sending their children regularly to school, and fines inflicted by the Magistrate amounted to £7 10s.

A TRUANT'S SPENDING SPREE

The story of one truant is told in the log book for 1895 of St Paul's Church of England Combined Schools, Leamington Spa:

> April 20/21 William W having stolen 5/6d from his mother played truant . . . . His mother brought him to school next morning and he accounted for his money as follows — 2 oranges 2d, 2nd class railway fare from Nuneaton to Coton and return 2d, biscuits 2d, Ginger Ale 1d, Pork pie 4d, fare to Tamworth and back 1/-, stamps 7d, chocolates 2d, Lucky Boys 1d, sherbert 2d, chewing gum 1d, cup of coffee 1d, cup of tea 2d, fried fish 2d, theatre 6d, sandwiches 2d, hose 1/-. He was caned at school and kept in at dinner time without his dinner.

He seems to have had rather good value for his money, though!

By May, William was expelled, for in one day he threw his dinner around the room, was rude to the teacher and broke some windows. The Vicar was called in to lecture to the whole school on the evils of bad behaviour.

◁ *This etching from the* Illustrated London News *of 1871 shows Lord Shaftesbury and members of the London School Board searching for truants — many of whom were probably also homeless and apart from their family. You can see how wretched the state of some children still was.*

Reading

As one of the "Three Rs", Reading was one of the most important subjects taught in a Victorian school. In Sunday Schools, children were taught to read from the Bible, but as schools became more wide-spread, easier methods were introduced. Children were taught to read first by identifying the alphabet, then by recognizing words of two letters, three letters, two syllables, and so on, until they could cope with whole paragraphs and texts. They were then given a "reader", which was a book full of short stories, poems and fables. A reader had to last for a whole standard, and so, if you finished it before the year was up, you just had to read it again, and again. Stories were often read aloud round the class, each child following the text with his finger.

READING FOR THE DIFFERENT STANDARDS

This list of reading books and poetry for the different standards was found in the log book for 1884 of St Paul's Church of England Combined Schools, Leamington Spa:

Standard I — Two Royal Readers and twenty lines 'The boy who told a lie'.
Standard II — Two Royal Readers and 40 lines 'The dog at his master's grave'.
Standard III — One Royal Reader, one historical and one geographical. 60 lines 'Lay of the brave man'.
Standard IV — One Royal Reader, one historical and one geographical. 80 lines 'Legend of the heart of Bruce'.
Standard V — School newspaper, one historical and geographical.
Poetry — Paradise Lost.

The poems, or parts of the poems, had to be learned by heart.

THE CONTENTS OF READERS

Special readers were designed for each Standard. The stories and poems in the readers either had a strong moral message or were meant to be "educational", or in some cases both. Here are some examples of titles:

Winter at Hand
Christmas Eve
The Avalanche
Heroism of Albert
Poverty
Relief
The Haymakers
The Telescope
Ironing Day
God provideth for the Morrow.

AN EASY LESSON OF ONE SYLLABLE

Here is Lesson 1 from Mavor's *Illustrated Spelling Book,* 1872:

I knew a nice girl, but she was not good; she was cross and she told fibs. One day she went out to take a walk in the fields, and tore her frock in a bush; and when she came home she said she had not done it, but that the dog had done it with his paw. Was that good? No. Her aunt gave her a cake, and she thought if John saw it, he would want a bit; and she did not choose he should; so she put it in a box, and hid it, that he might not see it. The

THE ENGLISH ALPHABET.

J j — Jay
K k — King
L l — Lion
m — Miser
N n — Nurse
O o — Owl
P p — Pig
Q q — Queen
R r — Raven

◁ *Part of an alphabet for infants from* Mavor's Illust-rated Spelling Book.

A POEM FOR 9-10 YEAR-OLDS

Oh say what is this thing called Light,
Which I must ne'er enjoy?
What are the blessings of the sight?
Oh tell a poor blind boy!

You talk of wondrous things you see,
You say the sun shines bright;
I feel him warm, but how can he
Or make it day or night?

My day or night myself I make
Whene'er I sleep or play;
And could I always keep awake,
With me 'twere always day.

With heavy sighs I often hear
You mourn my hapless woe;
But sure with patience I can bear
A loss I ne'er can know.

Then let not what I cannot have
My cheer of mind destroy;
Whilst thus I sing, I am a king
Although a poor blind boy.

next day she went to eat some of her cake but it was gone; there was a hole in the box, and a mouse had crept in, and eat it all. Oh dear, how she did cry! The nurse thought she was hurt; but when she told her what the mouse had done, she said she was glad of it; and that it was a bad thing to wish to eat it all, and not give a bit to John.

This exercise would have been used by seven and eight years olds. Notice that it has a strong moral message.

This comes from a selection of poetry in *Murby's Consecutive Narrative Reader,* Book 3, by Catherine Morell, 1879. The poem would have been recited and even learnt by heart by nine and ten year-olds. The subject is a fairly common one in Victorian literature and was intended to make children aware that there were many more unfortunate children than themselves. This poem, in fact, is unusually optimistic.

Writing and Spelling

The Victorians also paid much attention to good handwriting, another of the "Three Rs". The style used was formal and attractive and known as copperplate. Handwriting had to be clear and legible, for until the typewriter became widely available (in the 1870s) everything had to be handwritten. All children had to write with their right hand, even if they were left-handed.

Written work was done on sand trays, slates, and, for older children, in copybooks. Slates had several advantages — they were cheap, and could be used over and over again. Children were expected to bring their own sponges or bits of cloth to clean them with, but many relied on the "spit and cuff" method.

Spelling was considered very important and tests were frequent. Composition was introduced fairly late in the century, but Dictation was always a popular subject among teachers.

If the school could afford them, copybooks were given to children once they were past the slate stage. Children literally copied down the letters or words that were printed in the book. This is a page from a copybook belonging to A.J. Hewitt in 1887. Can you see which are the copied lines as opposed to the original ones? Try copying a sentence yourself — it is much harder than it looks. This copybook would have been for children in the first standard — aged about seven or eight.

The expression "to blot your copybook" comes from this period. What did it mean originally? And what does it mean today?

A tray of inkwells. Once they had a copybook, children were expected to write with pens. Inkwells were filled and distributed by a special monitor. Desks often had special holes for them.

SPELLING EXERCISES

Here are some examples of exercises in spelling from the *Girls' First Reader*, 1878. They were for six or seven year-olds. How would you do?

Med-dle	mor-sel	nee-dle
mel-low	mor-tar	neigh-bour
mem-ber	moth-er	net-tle
mer-chant	moun-tain	nib-ble
mer-cy	mud-dle	non-sense
mer-it	mur-der	nos-tril
mes-sage	mur-mur	noth-ing
met-al	mu-sic	no-tice
mid-dle	mus-tard	num-ber
mill-er	mut-ton	nut-meg
min-gle	muz-zle	oat-meal
mis-chief	na-ked	ob-ject
mi-ser	nap-kin	o-dour
mod-el	nar-row	of-fer
mod-est	nas-ty	off-spring
mo-ment	na-ture	oint-ment
mon-key	naught-y	ol-ive
mon-ster		

The words are split by a hyphen. Why do you think this was? Try saying the words yourself with a pause at the hyphen. This might give you a clue.

THE TEACHERS' COMPLAINTS

Extracts from the log books of St Paul's Church of England Combined Schools, Leamington Spa, reveal the teachers' dissatisfaction with the children's writing and spelling:

October 7 1863 Examined the younger hands and found in general the letters in writing ill-formed and uneven.

April 14 1866 The sixth Standard unable to spell Sepulchre and Synagogue in Dictation.

May 23 1866 Several boys in the Third Standard unable to spell father and water, given as 'farther' and 'warter'.

April 14 1867 In Dictation (the Third Standard) Soap, Soda and Coffee in every case spelt wrongly.

February 14 1868 One boy in Standard I unable to make a capital K.

'Rithmetic

The last of the "Three Rs" was Arithmetic. Victorians considered the Four Rules of Arithmetic (addition, subtraction, multiplication and division) to be the most important aspects of the subject. Small children were taught to add and take away on an abacus, while older pupils had special text books. It was essential to know times-tables off by heart, and mental arithmetic was "found to be a great stimulus to [children] hitherto backward". Victorian children also learnt about decimals, vulgar fractions, interest, percentages, weights and measures, time and capacity, as well as Mathematics (Algebra and Geometry).

Mixed questions like these were very popular in schools and are not as complicated as they may first appear. These were for Standard I (aged seven to eight). How many can you do?

MIXED QUESTIONS.

1. Tom had 264 marbles; he gave 64 to James, 75 to William, and 42 to John; how many had he left?

2. A merchant had 4268 yards of cloth; on Monday he sold 146 yards, on Tuesday 97, on Wednesday 246, on Thursday 198, on Friday 364, on Saturday 497; how much cloth had he remaining?

3. Three regiments went to battle; in the first there were 968 soldiers, in the second 769, and in the third 847. There were 248 men killed in the first regiment, 368 in the second, and when the regiments returned there were only 436 men in the third; how many returned from the battle?

4. A man had a journey of 298 miles to make; the first day he walked 42 miles, the second 36 miles, the third 31 miles, the fourth 27 miles; how much farther had he to go?

5. Three vessels sailed to America with emigrants; in the first vessel there were 126 men, 96 women, and 42 children; in the second vessel there were 93 men, 37 women, and 26 children; in the third vessel there were 43 men, 24 women, and 8 children. In the first vessel three persons died; in the second two were washed overboard; the third vessel was wrecked, and all on board perished; how many got safe to America?

6. A little boy went to the Zoological Gardens to see the animals; he laid his hat on the ground, which contained 264 nuts; while his attention was engaged, the monkey stole 27 of his nuts; while he was pursuing the monkey, a squirrel made off with 16 more; how many had he remaining?

7. The population of Cork was some years ago 108,000; of Belfast 55,000; of Liverpool 166,000; of Glasgow 203,000; by how much does the population of London exceed all these cities, the population of it being 1,776,556 in the year 1831?

8. Received on Monday £247; paid away on Tuesday £196; received on Wednesday £349; paid away on Thursday £402; received on Friday £687; paid away on Saturday £598; what money had I still remaining?

Numeration tables showed how to write numbers in letters and words. These exercises were for Standard I. See if you can do the more difficult ones.

NUMERATION TABLE.

1	Units
2 1	Tens
,3 2 1	Hundreds
4 ,3 2 1	Thousands
5 4 ,3 2 1	Tens of Thousands
,6 5 4 ,3 2 1	Hundreds of Thousands
7 ,6 5 4 ,3 2 1	Millions
8 7 ,6 5 4 ,3 2 1	Tens of Millions
,9 8 7 ,6 5 4 ,3 2 1	Hundreds of Millions
1 ,9 8 7 ,6 5 4 ,3 2 1	Billions
2 1 ,9 8 7 ,6 5 4 ,3 2 1	Tens of Billions
,3 2 1 ,9 8 7 ,6 5 4 ,3 2 1	Hundreds of Billions
4 ,3 2 1 ,9 8 7 ,6 5 4 ,3 2 1	Trillions

ROMAN NOTATION.

M.	D.	C.	L.	X.	V.	I.
1000	500	100	50	10	5	1

EXERCISES IN NUMERATION.

Read, or write down in words, the numbers signified by following figures:

1. 1, 2, 3, 4, 5, 6, 7, 8, 9, 0.
2. 10, 11, 14, 16, 19, 20, 42, 18, 17.
3. 200, 420, 607, 986, 473, 247, 364.
4. 912, 874, 783, 650, 202, 604, 510.
5. 4000, 2700, 8601, 7036, 2101, 1060.
6. 1010, 7020, 4600, 9111, 4076, 5870.
7. 26012, 70101, 42100, 36100, 90201.
8. 700000, 701020, 926427, 104206.
9. 9000000, 9764268, 8202100, 5023067.
10. 2600060, 4101010, 2004000, 1402149.
11. 40000000, 29602687, 50026017, 1670020.
12. 941268767, 267602607, 401467680.
13. 296026876, 710020010, 270603050.
14. 1402360740, 3460760010, 4023601497.
15. 7042602744, 5079607906, 1704070600.
16. 81462306012, 46007687681, 94086421360.
17. 14023641201, 20860002001, 40002000202.
18. 907060206204, 240026100201, 590960126020.

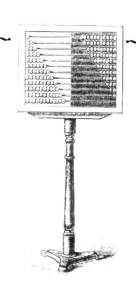

An abacus was a counting frame on which children ▷
could do simple addition and subtraction by moving
the beads along the wires. These are still used in some
junior schools today.

ACCOUNT KEEPING

Emphasis was put on account keeping, especially for
girls who would eventually have to manage their own
household accounts. The following two bills were
taken from the *First Book of Arithmetic, for use in
Schools,* 1870. The children had to calculate what the
total would come to.

Grocer's Bill
Mrs Young
July 16 1836   Bought of John Dicksoe
                                                       £   s   d
12lbs loaf sugar @ . . . .   10 per lb
9lbs green tea @   2   0   ”
6lbs Turkey coffee @   2   6   ”
8lbs Hyson tea @   8   6   ”
16lbs soft sugar @   8   ”
14lbs rice @   4   ”
15lbs currants @   11   ”
        Total: . . . .

Woollen Draper's Bill
Mr Thomas Sage   Bought of Ellis Smith
                                                       £   s   d
17yds fine serge @   3   9 per yard
10yds drugget @   9   0   ”
15yds superfine scarlet @   22   0   ”
16yds black cloth @   18   0   ”
25yds shalloon @   1   9   ”
17yds drab cloth @   17   6   ”
        Total: . . . .

These bills are also interesting because they tell you a
good deal about Victorian shopping. How many of
those materials do you recognize?

Other Subjects

After 1867 subjects other than the "Three Rs" became eligible for grants, and so the curriculum was slowly widened to include subjects such as Geography, History and Object Lessons. By 1902 the curriculum in most schools, especially Secondary Schools, was much more varied. (See pages 20-21 for more information.)

OBJECT LESSONS

Object Lessons were very popular. A particular object would be discussed and certain facts learnt by heart. If possible, the teacher would give out an example of the object to each child, as a visual aid. If the real object was not obtainable, posters or pictures were used. Here is a list of some of the Object Lessons taught in 1896-97 at St Paul's Church of England Combined Schools, Leamington Spa:

Standard I: Cat, mouse, sheep, hen, dog, rabbit, turnips, sparrow, buttercup, ivy, greenpeas, wheat, herbs, iron and metal, coffee, slate, birch, needles, paper, chalk, donkey, knife, fly, wasp, sunflower, rose, coal, a fire.

Standard III: Snail, butterfly, silkworm, coal, daffodil, sweet pea, solids, liquids, action of water on common things, crystal, spider, daisy, birds, silver, gold, mercury, iceberg, glacier, stream, the work of rivers, camel, teeth and their uses, paws and claws, rooks, how plants live, cocoa, ants, fur and wood, fruit and coal gas.

As you can see, the subjects were very diversified.

HISTORY

History was learnt in a question-and-answer manner. Information was often very biased towards the British Isles and the Empire.

Here are some examples from a book called *Simple Catechism of the History of England, from the Invasion of the Romans to the Present Time* by a Mrs Gibbon in 1891. This would be used in Standard I.

Chapter I, on the Invasion of Britain by the Romans

Q. When did Britain generally become known to the rest of Europe?

A. When it was invaded by the Romans, under Julius Caesar about fifty three years before the birth of our Lord Jesus Christ.

Q. In what state were the Britons at this time?

A. In a very rude state, wearing no clothes, and only a piece of woollen cloth around the waist.

Q. What sort of houses had they?

A. They were only mud huts or cottages.

Q. How long were the Romans masters of Britain?

A. About four hundred years, during which time the Britons improved greatly in all kinds of learning . . .

This infants class, photographed at the turn of the ▷ century, was having an Object Lesson about a small apple.

General Knowledge was also encouraged and again it was taught on a question-and-answer basis. This example is from a book called *The First Steps to Knowledge:*

Q. To what country do we owe the potato?
A. North America.
Q. Who first discovered this vegetable?
A. Sir Francis Drake.
Q. In whose reign?
A. That of Queen Elizabeth.
Q. Who first planted potatoes in Ireland?
A. Sir Walter Raleigh.
Q. In what year?
A. In 1610.
Q. Was this the reign of Queen Elizabeth?
A. No, that of James I.

Victorian children were learning by a different method from children today. Do you think the content of the lessons was very different too?

OUTLINES OF GEOGRAPHY.

THE earth is of the form of a globe or ball; its circumference is 360 degrees—each degree $69\frac{1}{2}$ statute miles, or 60 geographical miles; that is, nearly 25,000 miles in circumference, and nearly 8,000 miles in diameter. Its surface is composed of land and water; the land is divided into five great divisions, *Europe, Asia, Africa, America,* and *Australasia.*

The LAND consists of continents, islands, peninsulas, isthmuses, promontories, capes.

A CONTINENT is a large tract of land, embracing several kingdoms or states, not separated by seas; as Europe, Asia, Africa, America, and Australia.

An ISLAND is a smaller tract of land, entirely surrounded by water; as Great Britain, Ireland, &c.

A PENINSULA is a tract of land surrounded by water, except at one narrow neck, by which it is joined to the neighbouring continent

An ISTHMUS is the narrow neck of land by which the Peninsula is joined to the main land.

A PROMONTORY is an elevated point of land stretching into the sea, the end of which is called a cape.

The WATER is divided into oceans, seas, lakes, gulfs, straits, and rivers.

An OCEAN is a large tract of water not divided by any land.

A SEA is a smaller tract of water.

A GULF, or BAY, is a part of a sea running into the land.

A STRAIT is a narrow passage in the sea.

A LAKE is a tract of water entirely surrounded by land.

A RIVER is a stream of water, rising in the land and flowing into the sea.

The LAND is divided chiefly into two great continents, besides islands, the *Eastern* and *Western* Continents.

The EASTERN CONTINENT comprehends Europe, on the north-west; Asia, on the north-east; and Africa, joined to Asia by the isthmus of Suez, which is only sixty miles in breadth, on the south.

The WESTERN CONTINENT consists of North and South America, united by the isthmus of Darien, which, in the narrowest part, is only about thirty miles across.

A page from a book for Standard I, called Outlines of Geography. *Children would be expected to learn each fact by heart and answer correctly when questioned.*

Recreational Subjects

SINGING

On 16 October 1876 the log book of St Paul's Church of England Combined Schools, Leamington Spa, Warwickshire, lists twelve songs which had been prepared for the School Inspector. He chose to hear the sixth and the twelfth.

1. Men of Harlech
2. See our Oars
3. Scatter Seeds of Kindness
4. Scatter the Germs of the Beautiful
5. The Reaper's Song
6. The Fisher Boy's Song
7. The Poor Man's Garden
8. Always Cheerful
9. Roses Red
10. The Bonnie May
11. Star of Peace
12. Come the Summer now is Here

A little exercise was considered to be a good thing, for the Victorians believed in the saying "A healthy body for a healthy mind". Drill was usually included in the curriculum and was often taught by an ex-Army man, performed in a suitably military manner. Games such as cricket and rugger were not usually played at Elementary Schools. Singing was universal and was a grant subject. Children sang for the Inspector on examination day. Drawing was also popular, but children were all expected to draw the same thing in the same way, so there was little room for imagination. Girls were expected to be able to sew and were taught to make things that would be useful in later life.

How many of these do you know?

This sampler was worked by a girl in the seventh Standard, Yelvertoft School, Northamptonshire. Can you find her name and the name of her school? Samplers were done in order to practise a variety of stitches and sewing skills.

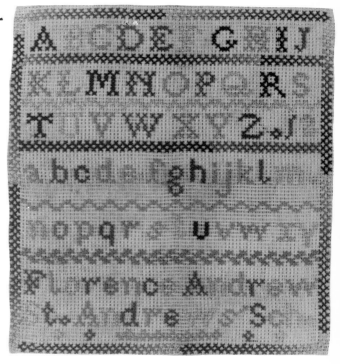

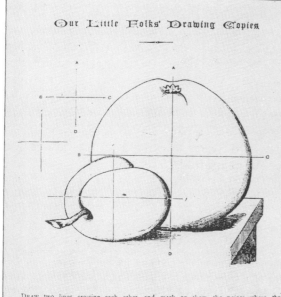

A simple drawing exercise from a magazine published in 1870, called Little Folks. Notice that the drawing was done by careful measuring and straight lines, which were later to be rubbed out. Would this technique be used today? What do we call our drawing methods today?

◁ These girls at Leicester Street Board School (for girls and infants), founded in 1884, seem to be wearing their best clothes for doing drill. This may have been for the photographer's benefit. Even so, there were no special PE kits, and so exercises must have been very difficult and hot. Exercises were usually done with sticks, dumb-bells and weights. The photograph was taken in the late 1890s.

DRAWING

Children were expected to copy and reproduce what they saw on the board, in the copybook or in front of them. At first, children learned how to draw simple shapes; they then progressed to patterns; and finally to objects. Drawing copybooks were used in a similar way to writing copybooks.

The St Paul's Church of England Combined Schools, Leamington Spa, log book recorded the results of a drawing examination:

> May 15 1878 The drawing examination took place on Monday morning. 163 papers were worked; 152 first grade, freehand; 6 second grade freehand; 2 second grade geometry; and two second grade model. Several children were absent on account of ringworm.

"Freehand" meant copying by eye, without using a ruler. "Geometry" meant drawing geometric shapes such as cubes and squares. "Model" involved drawing a specific object, from a plant to a person to a ball.

Holidays and Treats

Although most of the time was spent in long, and often boring hours in the classroom, the Victorian schoolchild could look forward to a good few weeks' annual holidays, the occasional half-day off and a treat once or twice a year, organized by the school.

THE SCHOOL YEAR, ST PAUL'S CHURCH OF ENGLAND COMBINED SCHOOLS

The log book of St Paul's School in Leamington Spa lists the following holidays and days off for 1865:

> Every Thursday a half holiday, Saturday a whole holiday. Two weeks at Christmas, two weeks at Easter. Whit Monday and Whit Tuesday [off]. Six weeks at Harvest.

Remember that most children were expected to attend Sunday School. How does this compare with your own holidays?

A Christmas Treat at a Ragged School in the mid-nineteenth century. The hall is festooned with holly and the children are scrubbed and in their best clothes.

This photograph was taken in 1910 at Cubbington School, Warwickshire. It shows a village May Day procession assembling in the school playground. Notice that the girls are in their best frocks, with flowers in their hats and garlands in their hands. A procession such as this went through the village and may have received gifts from villagers. There may have been a fair and maypole dancing, as well as the choosing of a May Queen.

HALF-DAY HOLIDAYS

Log books record a variety of reasons for half-day holidays. These extracts are all from the log books of St Paul's Church of England Combined Schools, Leamington Spa:

> April 24 1863 Half holiday in the afternoon, result of William B's success at examination. Took the First Division of the First Class to Kenilworth Castle, spent the afternoon in viewing the ruins and cricketing.

March 11 1870 Marriage of Princess Louise. Half holiday.

May 7 1876 There was no school on Friday afternoon as the room was required for Confirmation candidates to meet in prior to going to St Mary's Church.

October 1 1898 Holiday all day on account of Barnum and Bailey's Great Show.

SPECIAL TREATS

Special treats were organized for the children, usually twice a year, at Christmas and Harvest. Sometimes unique occasions also called for celebrations. The log books of St Paul's Church of England Combined Schools, Leamington Spa, record:

March 10 1863 Celebration of the Prince of Wales' Marriage. Children walked in procession through the town and sat down to dinner afterwards, numbering 280 . . . . Behaviour good and the affair passed pleasantly. Children sang and dismission followed.

May 1 1864 May Day. A few boys out with garlands.

December 7 1870 Magic Lantern at the Congregational School. Tickets given to several children of this school.

July 21 1876 On Wednesday afternoon the children of the Day and Sunday Schools, accompanied . . . by their teachers, were taken to Stoneleigh Park in breaks and vans. Tea was served about 5pm, preceded and followed by various games. All enjoyed themselves greatly and arrived home safely about 9pm.

February 7 1893 This afternoon a Punch and Judy entertainment was given to the boys and girls with the permission and at the expense of the Vicar.

December 1899 School broke up for the Christmas holidays . . . . Various games were played and nuts and oranges scrambled for . . . . Christmas cards were given away, each boy receiving one.

How to Identify a Victorian School

Most Victorian Schools, whether they date from the early or latter part of the nineteenth century, are very distinctive in appearance. First, examine your own school. It might appear to be modern, but does it have an earlier core? Clues to look out for generally include:

—Stone buildings, often church-like. Some are very bleak and plain, while others revel in the "gothic" style and are very flamboyant.

—High windows, so that the children couldn't look out.

—Plaques on the walls, giving either the date when the school was built, or the name of the school, or who it was built by, or all three.

—Bell towers and clock towers. Remember, children were summoned to school by bells.

—Street and house names — look out for things such as Old School Lane, School Cottages, etc.

Remember that almost every village had an Elementary School by the end of the nineteenth century, and many towns had examples of all the sorts of school mentioned in this book. Many schools are still in use. Others still exist, though in a different guise. They may now be used as private homes, or as commercial warehouses, or as community centres. The inevitable number are sadly empty or even derelict. Keep your eyes open and you are almost certain to find a Victorian school within a reasonable distance from your home. Good hunting!

Milverton Board Schools, Warwickshire. An ornate plaque gives the date of this school.

Ufton Village School, Warwickshire, now converted into two cottages.

Ettington School, Warwickshire, showing the clock tower. Can you also see the bell? When this photograph was taken, this school was up for sale.

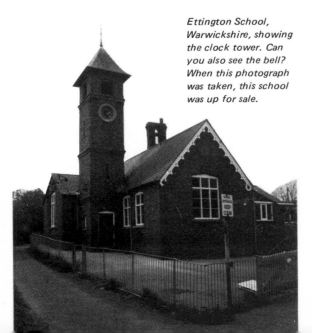

Bath Place National Schools, Leamington Spa. This school is now used as a community centre. Do you recognize it as the very smart National School from page 7?

Biographical Notes

ARNOLD, Thomas (1795-1842) Born on the Isle of Wight, Arnold was educated at Winchester and Corpus Christi College, Oxford. In 1828 he became Headmaster of Rugby School, where he instituted a firm but fair, Christian and gentlemanly regime. The boys under his care earned the reputation of being "thoughtful, manly-minded and conscious of duty and obligation". He did much to restore and enhance the reputation of the Public School system. He died suddenly in 1842, having published many books on historical and religious subjects.

BEALE, Dorothea (1831-1906) Miss Beale did much to make education for girls respectable and desirable. In 1857 she became Headmistress of the Clergy Daughters' School, Westmoreland and from 1858-1906 was Principal of the Cheltenham Ladies' College. The latter was run on similar lines to a boys' public school, with firm discipline, a wide-ranging curriculum and emphasis on academic results. She also helped found St Hilda's College, Cheltenham, for women secondary teachers and St Hilda's Hall, Oxford, for women.

FORSTER, William (1818-1886) Reared as a Quaker, Forster entered the woollen business in Bradford in 1841. In 1861 he was elected MP for Bradford and became concerned with reform and the plight of the poor. He is most renowned for his Education Act of 1870 which introduced School Boards responsible for the building of many new schools. In his later years he became involved with the Irish Problem and several attempts were made on his life. He died in 1886 and was given a funeral in Westminster Abbey.

KAY-SHUTTLEWORTH, Sir James (1804-1877) Born in Lancashire, he trained as a medical student and became a respected physician. In 1835 his concern with the health of the poor led him to become a Poor Law Commissioner. In 1839 he became Secretary to the newly formed Committee of Council for Education and was responsible for introducing the Pupil Teacher System, and for founding the first Teacher Training College. In 1849 he resigned due to bad health, but continued writing pamphlets and articles on education.

LANCASTER, Joseph (1778-1838) Brought up as a Quaker, he established his own free school for pauper children and introduced the "Lancasterian System" which used older children, or Monitors, to teach smaller groups of younger children. This form of teaching was used by the Royal Lancasterian Society, founded in 1810, which later became the British and Foreign Schools Society. This Society built British Schools, which were in direct competition to the National Schools of the Church of England. Lancaster quarrelled with other members of the Society and, disillusioned and badly in debt, he emigrated to America in 1818. He died in New York in 1838 as the result of a road accident.

MORANT, Sir Robert (1863-1920) Tutor to the Royal Family in Siam, in 1895 he was asked to make reports to the Board of Education on the education system of France, Switzerland and England. He is most remembered for his Education Act of 1902 which amalgamated Elementary and Secondary Schools under one administrative body, and introduced Local Education Authorities, which replaced the old School Boards. From 1903-1911 he was Secretary of the Board of Education, and ended his career as Secretary for the Ministry of Health.

Places to Visit

St John's House, Warwick — a branch of the County Museum. This contains a reconstruction of a Victorian schoolroom using authentic furniture and equipment. It is available to school parties.

Sudbury Hall, Derbyshire. Here also there is a functional schoolroom where Victorian lessons are conducted in a suitable manner.

Brewery Yard Museum, Nottingham contains a small, visual display.

Shugborough Hall, Staffordshire, has, amongst other things, a display showing a Victorian classroom.

Museum of London contains exhibits on the 1870 Act and Board Schools and has a Victorian classroom.

Castle Museum, York has a reconstruction of a schoolroom.

Difficult Words

abacus	wooden frame with beads, used for arithmetic.
Assistants	uncertificated teachers.
blue stocking	nickname given to women who were interested in learning, including teachers.
Board School	school set up by a local School Board.
British School	school founded by the British and Foreign Schools Society.
burgess	inhabitant of borough, with special municipal powers.
certificate	document given to a child on passing an exam; also a document given to a teacher on passing training.
Charity School	school set up by benefactor for poor children.
composition	a written piece of work on a given subject.
copperplate	the style of writing taught in schools and therefore used by the majority of people who could write.
copybook	workbook in which children copied printed sentences, to practise handwriting.
curriculum	the range of subjects taught.
Dame School	small school run by an elderly woman.
denominational	belonging to particular religious sect.
deportment	posture; the way a person walks and carries him/herself.
dictation	an exercise where children write down sentences read aloud by the teacher.
drill	type of Victorian P.E.
gallery	teaching room arranged on a slope.
Higher Grade School	Elementary School which had a 7th Standard, or a separate school for older children.
HMIs	Her Majesty's Inspectors.
log books	diaries kept by Head Teachers.
monitors	older children who passed on what they were taught to others in the class.
Pupil Teacher	child apprenticed to be a teacher.
Ragged School	school for very poor children.
Revised Code	code by which the annual Government grant to each school depended on attendance and examination results.
Royal Commission	inquiry into a national problem, sponsored by the Government. Findings are recorded in a Report.
sampler	piece of needlework on which stitches were practised.
school pence	weekly fee charged for each child, in all schools, including Board Schools. The fee varied from school to school and also depended on the financial state of the parents. The Board Schools charged 2d a week, but abolished the fees in 1891. The 1902 Act abolished school pence altogether.
slates	writing tablets.
standards	classes divided by age and ability.
State System	a system of education funded and legislated for by the State (i.e. the Government).
truant	child who purposely keeps away from school.
Voluntary School	a school paid for by gifts of money.
workhouse school	a school within a workhouse.

Date List

1780 First Sunday School opened by Robert Raikes.

1803 Joseph Lancaster's *Improvements in Education* published, describing the Monitorial System.

1810 Royal Lancasterian Society founded, which later became the British and Foreign Schools Society.

1811 The National Society for Promoting the Education of the Poor founded, establishing National Schools.

1818 First Ragged School opened by John Pounds.

1824 The Infant School Society founded by Robert Wilderspin.

1832 The Great Reform Act gives the middle class the vote.

1833 First Government grant awarded for the building of schools.

1834 Government report on *The State of the Education of the People.*

1839 Committee of Council for Education formed.

1840 First HMIs appointed.

1843 Factory Act introduces "half-time" system of education.

1844 Ragged School Union founded.

1846 Pupil Teacher system introduced.

1850 North London Collegiate School founded by Frances Buss.

1856 State Department of Education founded.

1858 Dorothea Beale becomes Headmistress of Cheltenham Ladies' College.

1861 Newcastle Report on Elementary Education published.

1862 Revised Code introduced.

1864 Clarendon Report on Public Schools.

1868 Public Schools Act. Taunton Report on Endowed Schools.

1869 Endowed Schools Act.

1870 Education Act introduces Board Schools.

1876 Minimum leaving age fixed at 10.

1880 Schooling compulsory up to the age of 10.

1888 Cross Report on Elementary Education.

1891 Elementary Education becomes free.

1895 Bryce Report on Secondary Education.

1897 Payment by Results abolished.

1902 Education Act replaces School Boards with Local Education Authorities.

Book List

Books for Younger Readers

Allen, Eleanor, *Victorian Children,* A. & C. Black, 1973

Dures, Alan, *Schools,* Batsford (Past-into-Present series), 1971

Ferguson, Sheila, *Growing up in Victorian Britain*, Batsford, 1977

Martin, Christopher, *A Short History of the English School,* Wayland

Seaborne, Malcolm, *Education,* Studio Vista

Speed, P.F., *Learning and Teaching in Victorian Times,* Longman, 1964

Wyand, John, *Village Schools, a future for the past,* Evans, 1980

Schools, Macmillan, (History Topic Series)

Try to read some of the chapters of the following novels:

Bronte, Charlotte, *Jane Eyre,* 1847 (chapters 5-10)

Dickens, Charles, *Nicholas Nickleby,* 1838-39 (chapters 7, 8, 9, 13)

Dickens, Charles, *Oliver Twist*, 1848

Hughes, Thomas, *Tom Brown's Schooldays,* 1857

Thompson, Flora, *Lark Rise to Candleford,* 1945 (chapters 11, 12)

Books for Teachers

Gadd, E.W., *Victorian Logs,* Brewin Books, 1977

Maclure, J. Stuart, Chapman and Hall, *Educational Documents 1816 — the present day*, Methuen, 1965

O'Shaugnessy, F., *A Spa and its Children,* Warwick Printing Company Ltd, 1979

Raistrick, Elizabeth, *Village Schools, an Upper Wharfedale History*, Daleman Publishing Company, 1971

Richardson, John, *The Local Historian's Encyclopedia,* Historical Publications, 1974

Walwin, James, *A Child's World*, Pelican, 1982

Education in Essex 1710-1910, Teaching Portfolio No 6, Essex Record Office

Index